Welcome to ffloe

At ffloe, we offer a new kind of travel book. We introduce carefully selected places, with suggestions on how to discover and enjoy them. We can be a guidebook, but we're much more than that.

We attempt as much as we can to capture visually the character, culture, heartbeat and history of a particular place. We believe that a picture really does tell a thousand words.

We focus on small areas, not vast regions or whole countries. We select them independently, looking for places which have beauty, values and opinions, and a twinkle in their eye – places that are fun. Places where there is a vitality, a sustainable community, and, crucially, a future. Where people take real pleasure in sharing and talking about the secrets behind this wealth, so that visitors, residents and the place itself can all benefit from the discovery. Some of your potential hosts in Dubrovnik and the Elaphites introduce themselves in pictures on the pages that follow.

If you are already in the area and want to take back with you a pictorial reminder of a wonderful experience, then this book is for you. If you are looking for a suggestion of a place to visit in the future, then this book will whet your appetite. There's enough here to plan a trip yourself. Alternatively, you can have it tailor-made for you by others, such as Original Travel (originaltravel.co.uk), our recommended independent travel partner. We offer plenty of other contacts as well.

Keep an eye on our website ffloe.com for further information and news. We welcome your feedback too, and of course let us know of any other places you think we should take a look at.

Travel is one of life's great pleasures. It uplifts and rejuvenates the soul. At ffloe, our aim is to help you make the most of it.

www.ffloe.com

Contents

Introducing Dubrovnik and the Elaphites

Dubrovnik is an incredible place; an architectural masterpiece that everyone should visit at least once in their lifetime. Its magnificent walls, marble streets and unique atmosphere were once one of Europe's best-kept secrets. Alas, no more. But what still remains largely unknown, except to the particularly well informed, is what lies just outside its gates, and, especially, beyond its rocky promontory.

Strung out offshore just to the north of the Old Town, running roughly parallel with the mainland, is an archipelago of 13 islands and islets. These are the Elaphites, for centuries the destination of choice for Dubrovnik's rich merchantmen, boat-builders, aristocrats, noblemen and their families. It was here that they built their summer villas and pleasure gardens: places for enjoyment, reflection and intellectual discourse during the golden age of the old Ragusan Republic. Surrounded by lush subtropical vegetation, warmed by endless summer sunshine and cooled by gentle sea breezes, these Renaissance playgrounds were a world away from the hustle and bustle of the city. They still feel that way today.

The largest three, Šipan (about the size of Capri), Lopud and Koločep are inhabited, though sparsely. They are special places with their own soul and values, rich in natural produce and heritage – as magical as ever. To find a place so utterly unspoiled anywhere in the world now is rare. To find it here, so close to the crossroads of Europe, and right by an international airport, is special indeed.

That's not a starter gun for tourism over-development, either. These islands are too logistically challenging for that. Also, the Croatian people are vigilant guardians of what they have: they are too smart to allow careless exploitation. (Ironically, the danger may be the opposite: too little done too slowly.)

Enjoy Dubrovnik and the Elaphites. Make it a journey. Be uplifted, encouraged and fascinated by what you see and those whom you meet. And above all, take your time.

Koločep

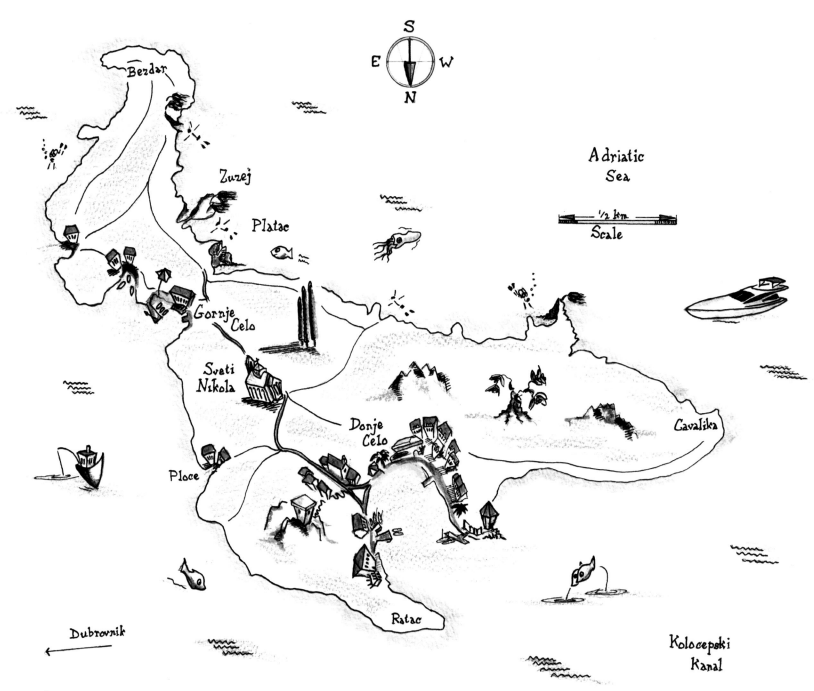

Bezdar

Zuzej

Platac

Adriatic
Sea

½ km
Scale

Gornje
Celo

Sveti
Nikola

Donje
Čelo

Cavalika

Ploce

Ratac

Dubrovnik

Kolocepski
Kanal

Koločep

Size: 2.35 sq km
Population: 200
Settlements: Donje Čelo and Gornje Čelo
High points: Križ (125m) and Spasovo Brdo (97m)

'Those who live in this place work the land and fare the sea,
All strive to thrive and prosper in their chosen path of life.
Not a soul steals or cheats since brethren we all are,
All follow their roads in peace, happiness and love.'

– Vlaho Skvadri

PAST UNINHABITED DAKSA, Koločep is the first stop for the ferry out of Dubrovnik. Today, it is something of a dormitory for the city, with commuters shuttling to and fro at the beginning and end of the day. That proximity, plus the deep, wide harbour of the main settlement, Donje Čelo – one of the best protected in the whole of Dalmatia and famed as a safe haven for centuries – has defined the history of this small island. Historically, its inhabitants have been particularly cultured, benefiting from the frequent visits of Dubrovnik sophisticates, and harbouring merchant ships from the whole of Ragusa, Venice, the Levant and beyond. Consequently, it was the first of the Elaphites to develop its own fleet, and so to prosper. It was also the first to decline.

Today, Donje Čelo is little more than a village: a tidy cluster of terracotta-roofed, mainly two-storey houses surrounded by greenery, trees and exotic gardens, sprinkled around the sweeping bay. It's an idyllic setting: the beach is largely sandy, ideal for swimming, and a rocky limestone ridge offers protection from the wind. There are few classic 'sights' here, but this is a great place for walking and general exploring. Just up from Donje Čelo's waterfront, an easy path heads off across the island, past old olive groves and vineyards (it's said that the first vine was planted here in the 13th century) with excellent views, to arrive in the small, pretty, if rather overgrown Gornje Čelo, nestling in its own bay on the southeast side of the island. From here, it's another easy walk down to beautiful, sandy Donđivan bay, a lovely, sheltered swimming spot, with calm, warm water and a gently shelving beach.

Historically, Koločep was always ahead of neighbouring Lopud and Šipan – in good times, and in bad. Its boom began in the 14th century, when it started to develop its merchant fleet, building around 37 ships which sailed across the Adriatic, all the way to Sicily, and Valona in southern Albania. It had no rival in the whole Republic, apart from Dubrovnik itself – Lopud and Šipan had a mere three large ships each at the time. The 15th century was its golden age, when many churches and fine summer residences were built, and fields and vineyards planted, by local families and also the great estate owners of Dubrovnik, such as

the famous families Đorđić, Ranjina, Držić and Sorgo, as well as the archbishops of Dubrovnik. By the mid-15th century its fleet had almost doubled to 65.

But it didn't last. Koločep was too successful, and its neighbours started to compete, first Lopud, then Šipan, then others, building newer, bigger, better boats. Its trade fell off a cliff, and by the 16th century, only a third of its fleet remained. Its population disappeared along with its prosperity, shrinking back to little more than 400 families. Abandoned by the Dubrovnik merchants, Koločep was too slow or too short of resources to modernise its own fleet. Desperate, they sold their worn-out ships and their captains looked for service with other fleets, maintaining their reputation for being brilliant sailors.

Koločep had other worries too. It had long been harrassed by pirates, from Dalmatia, Albania and Africa – and even a rogue Venetian, called Nikola Lavizolo, the 'bandito da Venezia', dubbed 'a completely wicked man' by local historian Vicko Lisičar, who pillaged part of the island, killing a number of inhabitants. Then, in 1571, a fleet of Turkish ships attacked Koločep, Lopud and Šipan, particularly devastating Koločep, prompting an upgrading and building of fortifications all around the island, notably a fortress on the west side, overlooking the harbor of St Cross. Today, the upper part is ruined, but the large subterranean chambers – 30 metres long and three metres wide – are still well preserved. In this underground space alone several hundred could hide while the enemy marauded outside. The remains of various other towers and fortifications are still visible around the island.

While Koločep's decline well preceded the general eclipse of the Republic, it was spared the devastation of the earthquake that struck Dubrovnik on 6 April 1667. Perhaps because its buildings were constructed on solid rock, Koločep escaped largely unscathed, and not a single inhabitant was killed. A much more potent destructive force on Koločep has been time and neglect, but this, as is the case across the Elaphites, is beginning to change. 🜛

Splendid isolation

Koločep is a great island for walking. A gentle path connects Donje Čelo (above left and top), set around a superb natural harbour, and pretty Gornje Čelo, with its lovely sandy beach on the southeast side. More paths strike out into the fragrant forests of the interior, or drop into isolated rocky bays – there is also a 'blue cave' to be explored by swimmers. Lush subtropical vegetation thrives in this climate: pines, cypresses, palms, agaves, cacti, vines, lemon, orange, olive, almond, carob (made into brandy) and more, plus orchids and medicinal herbs. For history, the island's early prosperity is reflected in its superb pre-Romanesque churches.

15

Lopud

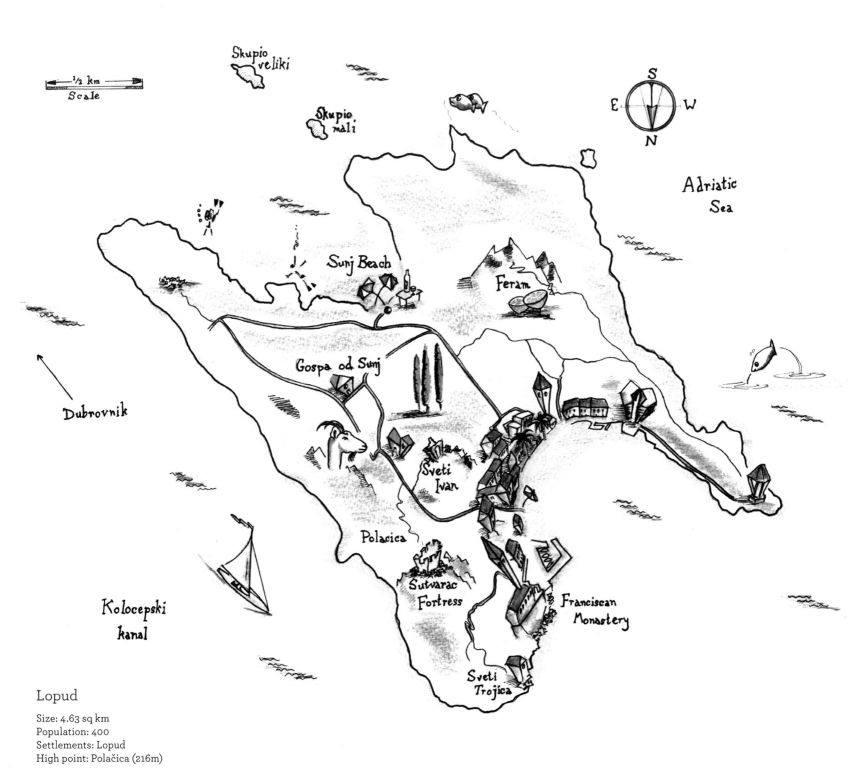

Skupio veliki

Skupio mali

Adriatic Sea

S
E · W
N

Sunj Beach

Feram

Gospa od Sunj

Dubrovnik

Sveti Ivan

Polacica

Sutvarac Fortress

Franciscan Monastery

Kolocepski kanal

Sveti Trojica

½ km
Scale

Lopud

Size: 4.63 sq km
Population: 400
Settlements: Lopud
High point: Polačica (216m)

'Is there anywhere more enjoyable to live!
Oh, crazy is everyone who touches your shores
Who may stay and he leaves.'

– Marko Bruerovic

SMALL, SLEEPY AND car-free though it is, Lopud is the most developed of the Elaphites – which just goes to show how unspoiled these islands are. It is also perhaps the most immediately appealing. It has just one village, also called Lopud, with pretty houses, some downright gorgeous Italianate villas, and lemon tree-filled gardens stacked neatly along the wide welcoming bay. There's a pleasant sandy beach, too, some terrific restaurants with views of Šipan that can be spellbinding, particularly at night, and a shady Renaissance garden that's ideal for a cool afternoon stroll.

At one end of the *passeggiata*-perfect esplanade stands a 15th-century Franciscan monastery; at the other, the communist-era Hotel Lafodia, looking rather like a pair of giant stacked heels, looking out to sea – a rare aberration that reminds you just how different all this could be. Above the harbour, on top of a hill, broods a ruined Ragusan fortress, and behind, a path strikes out across the island to Sunj, the pride of Lopud: a glorious sandy horseshoe beach that is without a doubt the best in the area, and a prime stop-off for passing yachts and flotillas.

Lopud is full of surprises. Witness the Franciscan monastery, which you pass as the ferry pulls into the harbour, its high fortified walls rising straight up from the edge of its rocky promontory at the edge of the bay. Formerly near derelict after years of neglect by cash-strapped authorities, it is currently being refurbished by Francesca von Habsburg, scion of the old ruling dynasty, as both a private residence, and a new outpost for her Thyssen-Bornenisza Art Contemporary (aka T-B A21) foundation (see page 21). T-B A21 is also working on reviving the monastery's Renaissance garden, drawing on historical descriptions of plants found in the scientific herbaria of medieval Franciscan Monks and commissioning French architects François Roche and Stéphanie Laveaux (R&Sie) to design a building for its upper terraces.

Another surprise awaits at the far end of the harbour in the shape of the stunning Grand Hotel, now sadly derelict although plans are afoot to refurbish this too. Looking like it belongs on Tracy Island rather than Lopud, it's astonishing to discover that it was actually built in 1936, on the back of a mini tourist boom that began here in the 1920s (see page 23). Between the Grand and La Villa, a charming boutique hotel that is one of the nicest places to stay in the whole Elaphites, is the start of the main path across the island to Sunj beach, a 15-minute walk away. Intriguingly, this was built by the Czech writer and politician Viktor Dyk, only for him to later drown nearby after suffering a heart attack while swimming.

Lopud is often called Insula Medio, the island in the middle, which holds true for its size, its location, and its historical development. Lopud had its maritime boom in between those of Koločep and Šipan. It outgrew Šipan's jurisdiction in 1457, becoming the seat of the new principality of Lopud and Koločep as the swelling Republic reorganised. Lopud built its own Rector's Palace to house its new governor: its remains, with beautiful windows in the Venetian style, surrounded by a garden and a high wall, can still be seen above the harbour. It was about this time that Lopud started building its own ships in earnest: caravelles that were bigger, more solidly built and more heavily armed than those of Koločep, notably those of the Pracatović family.

The ever-richer merchants and sailors started building churches and great houses, and Lopud began to attract Dubrovnik gentry too, swelling the summer population to some 4000. Many of those houses are now crumbling or ruined, such as the residence of the Ðordic family, but it is their gardens that make up that lovely Renaissance park. Like Koločep, Lopud was eclipsed in its turn by its bigger, more powerful neighbour, Šipan, particularly as the Skočibuhas started building their ever-mightier ships in the 16th century; and it too suffered from the decline of the Republic. But it was the first to recover, emerging as a smart tourist destination between the wars – a trend that continued during the communist era, and which is blossoming today. *ffi*

19

Surprise attraction

Lopud's Franciscan monastery (left) is currently being refurbished by Francesca von Habsburg, scion of the old ruling dynasty. It is becoming both a private residence, and a new outpost for her Thyssen-Bornenisza Art Contemporary (aka T-B A21), a dynamic organisation which is building 'an international network of pavilions' that promote contemporary art projects in 'remote environments'. It has already been the venue for various symposia attracting heavy-hitting international artists, academics and intellectuals. Nearby, almost in hiding, is the striking T-B A21-commissioned 'Your black horizon' Art Pavilion (right and bottom), which debuted at the Venice Biennale in 2005, then transferred here in 2007 for a three-year showing (but it's always possible that this might be extended).

21

Pleasure principles

Lopud's esplanade is studded with pretty houses and gorgeous Italianate villas. In the middle is the Đorđić-Mayner Park (opposite), a Renaissance garden full of exotic plants, pines, palms, and plenty of cool shade. A few steps beyond lies the ruined palace of Miho Pracat, the 16th-century merchant shipowner whose bust stands in the Rector's Palace in Dubrovnik. Lopud folk tales sought to explain how Pracat came by his fabulous wealth. He is said to have robbed Dubrovnik cathedral's treasury to pay for his business ventures, one of which involved exporting the city's cats to North Africa, where he had chanced upon a plague of rodents. Further on, by the path that leads to Sunj beach, is the Grand Hotel, a rare major work by Nikola Dobrović (left).

23

To the beach

Sunj (opposite) is a lovely spot, sheltered from the wind, with calm, gently shelving water, and snorkelling at both ends of the bay. From there you can keep walking and more or less circumnavigate the island, or branch off to visit the church of Our Lady of Sunj (below), built in the 15th century with 17th century additions, with an impressive churchyard outside and even more impressive paintings inside. The path arcs back into Lopud, coming out by the harbour.

Where to stay

The following listings cover Lopud and Koločep, both of which are undergoing renovation and change – particularly Lopud, as its appeal is increasingly publicised. Yet there is no sense they will be overwhelmed by mass tourism – these developments are carefully planned. The largest and most modern hotel, Lafodia, is actually reducing its room count as it undergoes major rebuilding to become a luxury hotel.

Kalamota Hotel Villas (Koločep) The island's only hotel, built in 1976 and renovated in 2006, with 151 rooms in eight villas and a swimming pool just next to the beach. Owned by the Island of Knowledge foundation, whose aim is a sustainable mix between the online world and the island's natural tranquility.
T: +385 (0)20 757025 W: kolocep.com

Villa Vilina (Lopud) Under new management since 2008, near neighbour to the Franciscan monastery at the mainland end of the bay, in an elevated position with views across the bay. The main building was originally a private house; there are further rooms and a pool across an open garden to the rear. Restaurant at the front with good views over the bay. T: +385 (0)20 759333 W: villa-vilina.hr

La Villa (Lopud) Situated close to Lopud's shoreline beach, it also backs on to the island's botanic garden. Owned by Francesca von Habsburg, this is a charming boutique hotel with well judged contemporary decor and great views straight on to the bay. The young couple who run it are extremely friendly – they also work for TB-A21, so they're very well informed on its art projects. Ask for the room with the roof terrace unless you're suspicious (it's room 13).
T: +385 (0)913 220126 W: lavilla.com.hr

Hotel Glavovic (Lopud) To the harbour end of the main waterfront, refurbished in 2004, with 10 bedrooms and two suites.
T: +385 (0)20 759359 W: hotel-glavovic.hr

Lafodia Hotel (Lopud) Modern-style building at the west end of the bay, currently undergoing refurbishment to become a luxury hotel.
T: +385 (0)20 759022 W: lafodiahotel.com

Rooms for rent There is currently no central accommodation agency or website for either Koločep or Lopud. Please refer to ffloe.com for further information and links.

Where to eat and drink

Villa Ruza (Koločep) Part of the Kalamota Hotel Villas, this has a glorious setting overlooking the length of Kolocepski Kanal, with its own jetty. A great place to watch the sunset or boats.
T: +385 (0)20 757025

Obala (Lopud) On the main waterfront, Ivo's fine restaurant serves fresh fish beautifully prepared. There are tables right on the waterfront, with stunning sunsets and a memorable atmosphere. People regularly boat over from the mainland and surrounding islands to eat here. Book in advance. T: +385 (0)20 759170

Villa Vilina (Lopud) Elevated views from the hotel's restaurant.

Tavern Peggy (Lopud) Up an alley behind the harbour, with a regular following of devotees. T: +385 (0)20 759036

Barbara's (Lopud) Family restaurant 100 metres or so back into the village from the waterfront with a terrace overlooking the bay.

T: +385 (0)20 759087

Konoba Dubrovnik (Lopud) Simple local spot. T: +385 (0)20 759172

What to do

Walks to Sunj and beyond It's an easy 15-minute walk to Sunj along the path that begins by the Grand Hotel, with some great views, particularly looking down on to the beach itself. Here, there are sun-loungers and umbrellas to rent, and a couple of cafes serving simple but delicious food, notably freshly caught fish.

From Sunj you can keep walking counter-clockwise around the island, more or less, arcing back into Lopud between two hills, with their own paths: one leads up to the **Ragusan fortress** and splendid views; and one up to **St Ivan/John**, one of four Croatian early Christian chapels on the island. Another, the sublimely simple and peaceful **St Nicholas**, is hidden in trees behind the fortress.

Alternatively, you can keep walking around Lopud bay, past Lafodia, to the viewpoint at the end – the perfect sunset spot – or continue along the upper path for more views over Lopud village, turning left to join the path to Sunj. Keep your eyes peeled for **bee orchids** in spring/early summer.

The Grand Hotel A rare major work by Nikola Dobrović, considered to be Serbia's most important modern architect and a major figure in modernism full stop. Trained in Prague, where he built a handful of small buildings, Dobrović settled in Dubrovnik in 1934, building various villas in the area, including Lopud: there's a striking example just past Hotel Lafodia, built in 1939, but again sadly in disrepair. What makes the Grand so rare is its scale: many of Dobrović's bigger projects were never executed, including his later work on urban planning in Belgrade. Clearly an exceptional building, even in its current dilapidated state, it is due to be refurbished. Not much you can do but look just now – but worth it.

'Your black horizon' Just off a path leading back from the esplanade, this Art Pavilion was designed by superstar London-based architect David Adjaye and contains a light installation by Danish artist Olafur Eliasson, known for such spectacular work as 'The Weather Project', the gigantic artificial sun that was such a hit at the Tate Modern's Turbine Hall. Catch it if you can – it's due to go at the end of the 2009 season.

ATMs Koločep: near the Kalamota Hotel Villas; Lopud: on the main bay near the Tourist Information Office.

Šipan

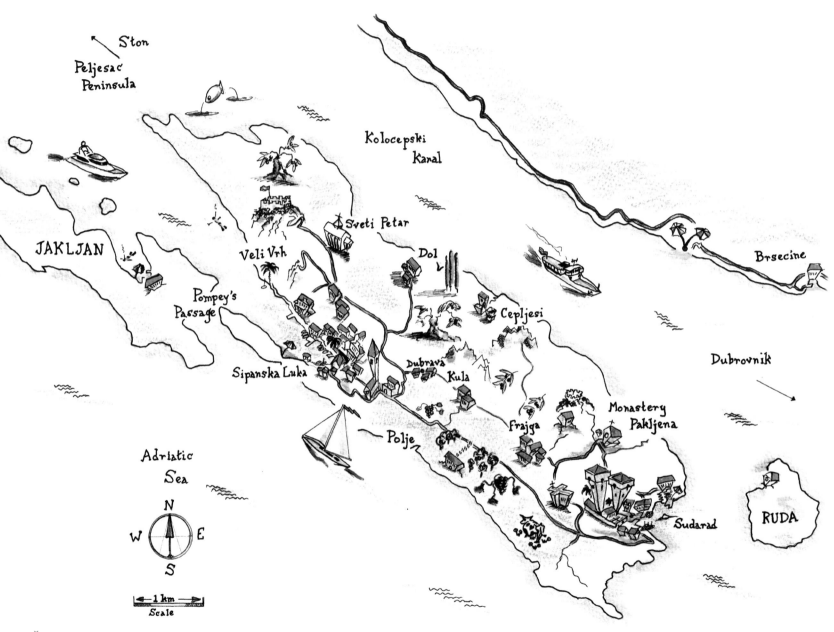

Ston

Peljesač
Peninsula

Kolocepski
Kanal

JAKLJAN

Sveti Petar

Veli Vrh

Dol

Brsecine

Pompey's
Passage

Cepljesi

Dubravà

Dubrovnik

Kula

Sipanska Luka

Frajga

Monastery
Pakljena

Adriatic

Polje

Sea

N

W   E

Sudarad

RUDA

S

1 km
Scale

Šipan

Size: 16.5 sq km
Population: 500
Settlements: Šipanska Luka and Suđurađ
High points: Velji Virh (243m) and St Ilija (223m)

*'They were all sleeping in the afternoon,
when I was approached by my lady,
"Let us enjoy the soothing shade
of our pleasure garden".'*

– Ignjat Durdevic

ŠIPAN HAS BEEN known as the Golden Island since classical times, and with good reason. The biggest, and most fertile of the Elaphites, its craggy hills fringe a central plain, or *polje*, that was once called the breadbasket of the Ragusan Republic – and is still thick with olive trees, vines and other crops today. It has a rich history, too, reflected in the 38 churches and chapels, and the 42 Renaissance summer villas that were built here – many of which can still be seen, some quite remote, surrounded by greenery in the sometimes exotic and wild interior, accessed via the sunken paths called 'roads' that criss-cross the island. This is an island with a slightly mysterious air; rather like it's full of secrets, waiting to be discovered.

The least developed of the Elaphites, Šipan has just two main settlements, both little more than villages, very pretty and steeped in history. Šipanska Luka is the largest, occupying a stunning spot at the end of a sheltered, island-studded bay that has long been popular with sailors. It has a sprinkling of good restaurants and local bars, and some lovely waterfront architecture – its grand, shuttered buildings give it a real Riviera flavour – capped by the Gothic-Renaissance splendour of the old Rector's Palace, high on the hillside.

Suđurađ, to the southeast, is a quiet fishing village, built around a harbour (where the ferry now stops) and dominated by two grand Renaissance villas, with friendly waterfront cafes and a main square, where children often play – all great spots to sit and watch the world go by. The two are connected by a tiny country road, which meanders across the *polje*, occasionally branching out to connect the various hamlets, such as Frajga, Sutulija, Vonjevo Selo and Ođak. These are very scenic and worth a visit, although many of the houses, built from local stone and with some lovely artisan details, are now abandoned and awaiting renovation.

Šipan is a timeless spot that has seen many civilizations come and go. It still has the remains of defensive walls that date back to ancient Illyrian times. It has been host to the Greeks, who called it Gypanon, or 'Eagle's Nest', and the Romans, who renamed it Tauris, after its outline which resembles the head of a bull. The Roman Villa Rustica still remains in Šipanska Luka, and it was just outside the harbour here that the fleets of Caesar and Pompey met in 47BC, as they chased across the Adriatic during their civil war. Pompey escaped through a narrow channel and out to sea, living to fight (and lose) another day. Locals today still call it 'Pompey's Passage' – it's just by the village's main beach, a thin strip of sand on the rocky outcrop at the far end of the west of the bay. (You can find other spots for a dip by following the path on the opposite side of the bay, flanked by the rocky shoreline and shady terraced olive groves.)

The Renaissance was Šipan's heyday, becoming the summer retreat of choice for Ragusa's thriving gentry. The Republic was by then a hotbed of creativity, freely exchanging ideas with the great Italian city-states, while artists, intellectuals and aristocrats travelled between them. Šipan was where the elite came to socialise and nurture their burgeoning love of art, building villas and palazzos, often with fantastic gardens and terraces covered by thick lattice to offer cool shade. Many of these residences are still here, in more or less their former glory, built by a roll call of the great local families: in Suđurađ, by Ranjina, Sagrojević and Getaldić (they bagged one of the best spots, on the sunny side of town, with a great view over Lopud); in Šipanska Luka, by Lukarević, Zamanja and Sorkočević.

As Ragusa's star waned, so Šipan's fortunes declined too, leading to generations of increasing economic inactivity. Once, Šipan's population stood at some 7000; now it is just 500. Ironically, it is this very decline that has preserved Šipan's natural beauty, and may well secure its future as it is rediscovered by those who appreciate its quiet charm. Slowly, Šipan is regenerating and locals are returning. The island now comes alive in summer again, when visitor numbers peak and local gatherings, sporting events and festivals are held, notably the Summer Film School, which took place for the fourth time in 2008. But mostly it draws those who appreciate its peace, its scenery and its uniquely unspoiled atmosphere. *ffi*

Renaissance men

Sudurad is still dominated by the summer residences (opposite, left, below) of the most important figures in Šipan's history: Tomo Skočibuha and his son Vice, who built up a successful shipyard and merchant fleet, and became among the wealthiest merchants and bankers in the Republic. Both true Renaissance men, they were great builders of churches, and patrons of the arts. They left many cultural and artistic monuments; their palazzos inside the city walls in Dubrovnik and at Boninovo were among the finest. They built fortress-like houses in Sudurad side by side, one in 1529, one in 1577 – the second added, it is said, because Vice's wife couldn't get on with her mother-in-law.

Lord of the Islands

Šipanska Luka is perhaps the most atmospheric spot in the Elaphites, with grand shuttered buildings and a stunning location set back in a long, deep harbour studded with green islands. The village actually originated on the hill hidden out of sight from marauding pirates. In the Middle Ages, this was effectively the capital of the archipelago: its Rector's Palace was the seat of the Comes Insularum, the Lord of the Islands.

Somewhere that's green

Criss-crossed by sunken paths called 'roads', Šipan is best explored on foot, with plenty of churches, palazzos and ancient olive groves to discover. There are very few cars on the island, and these belong to locals (the main ferry, Postira, only takes foot passengers). According to local folklore, the first two cars were bought by one man in Suđurađ and another in Šipanska Luka. One night, each had visited the other village for a good dinner. Returning home, they collided head-on, on the *polje*, roughly halfway between the two.

39

Wide renown

In its Ragusan heyday, Šipan's reputation spread beyond the Republic. Even King René of Anjou summered here: the ruins of his house can still be seen not far from Sveti Duh, at a site called Renatovo. But perhaps the most famous visitor was Cardinal Lodovico Beccadelli, a renowned humanist, writer and patron of the arts, whose portrait by Titian hangs in the Uffizzi. He came from Rome after being appointed Archbishop of Ragusa, and often spent time in the episcopal summer house (right) – called Biskupija – between Šipanska Luka and Suđurađ. Here, he corresponded regularly with Michelangelo, a great friend from his Rome days, even inviting him to stay. Too old to travel, the elderly artist declined, so Beccadelli had his face painted above the porch by a local artist instead, where it can still be seen.

Where to stay

There aren't that many hotel beds on Šipan, but there are also rooms for rent. Note that most of Šipan's hotels and restaurants close during the low winter season. Remember that the shoulder seasons are often the best times to visit.

Hotel Bozica A well-run small family hotel in a superb elevated position just outside Suđurađ, about a seven-minute walk from the village. Opened in 2007, Bozica is clean and tidy, with 26 rooms (including suites and some with balconies) and a restaurant. All the rooms and public areas, including the infinity pool, face the sea and have great panoramic views from Lopud to Suđurađ. You can swim directly off the hotel's own dock, where there are also sunbeds. Bozica has its own water taxi too.
T: +385 (0)20 325400/356829 **W:** hotel-bozica.hr 🛈

Šipan Hotel A mid-market hotel in Šipanska Luka that was originally a mill. With its own restaurant, it has no pool, and the rooms aren't large, but it occupies a commanding position at the head of the bay.
T: +385 (0)20 754900 **W:** hotel-sipan.com

Rooms for rent There is currently no central accommodation agency or website. Please refer to ffloe.com for further information and links.

Vukorep Agritourism Just behind Suđurađ, live in a rural household with meals provided. Three rooms. **T:** +385 (0)20 758024

Where to eat and drink

As with any of the Elaphites, food is the cornerstone of the Šipan way of life, and the island has quietly welcomed connoisseurs for a long while. Many well-known names pass through here.

Konoba Kod Marko On the waterfront at the far west end of the bay in Šipanska Luka, Marko's restaurant is a legend. Whilst Marko creates wonders in the kitchen, son Gino welcomes and serves you. The menu is whatever there is, mostly fish, and you can always count on a memorable lunch or dinner here. Enjoy Marko's octopus recipe, and if he is serving it, leave room for the orange cake... Book ahead.
T: +385 (0)20 758007/(0)98 608687 🛈

Tauris ('Miro's') In the heart of Šipanska Luka, Miro's is just as busy as Marko's, serving excellent seafood. There will be fish of the day (depending on the day's catch) and Miro also grills amazing steaks. Book in advance. **T:** +385 (0)20 758088 **W:** sipan.info 🛈

More ('Baldo's') Baldo runs a friendly open all-year waterfront konoba serving daily menus, much of which is based on locally sourced produce. **T:** +385 (0)989 426427

Bozo's Cafe Artist and philosopher Bozo will welcome you warmly. Located in the corner of Šipanska Luka. Open most days of the year.
No Name Cafe Yes, that's its name. Next to Bozo's.
Teo's Cafe Located on the waterfront in Suđurađ, Teo, family and friends are always welcoming, and open year round. A good first stop on arrival from the ferry, or while waiting to depart. Teo also has rooms for rent that are above the cafe in the heart of the village.
T: +385 (0)989 004143 **W:** dubrovnik-online.com/apartment_bogdan

Stara Mlinica ('Old Mill') Konoba in Suđurađ – a good place from which to watch the world go by. **T:** +385 (0)989 004143

Na Zalima Another konoba closer to the castle in Suđurađ. Locally sourced produce, especially cheese from the island's few cows.
T: +385 (0)20 758030

Na Taraci Recently opened in Suđurađ, at the castle's oil press, this is operated by Hotel Bozica. **T:** +385 (0)20 325400/356829

What to do

Walking Recommended as a great way to get to know the island at your own pace. You will see (and often smell) many varieties of flora – pungent herbs, orchids, ancient olive groves, vines, pines and cypresses – and constantly come across hidden architectural treasures. Some suggestions: 1. End to end across the *polje*, following the road (5.8 kilometres) between Suđurađ and Šipanska Luka (you can always take the bus back). 2. End to end via the hamlets of Frajge and Dubrava (as 1, but along a more elevated scenic path). 3. Napoleonic fort and Sv Peter: an uphill rigorous hike from Šipanska Luka, with amazing views. 4. Veli Vrh and above Šipanska Luka (as 3, but shorter). 5. Behind Suđurađ: an introduction to the island. 6. Šipanska Luka bay: waterfront tranquility on the level. 7. A la carte (a route of your own): discuss beforehand with a local, take care and water. For more details on these itineraries, visit ffloe.com.

Bikes You can go many places by bike, but not quite as many as on foot. Rental available at Suđurađ. **T:** +385 (0)989 348254

Fishing ...is excellent. Ask locally.

Olive Oil Buy some of the local oil, direct from the growers or look out for new dedicated brands which are being established for the island. Or adopt a tree of your own (see ffloe.com).

Šipan Film Festival Every summer. This is a film-based cultural festival, largely aimed at children, to introduce and develop those showing promise in the world of celluloid. **W:** sipan-film.com

Art Itea Gallery, in Suđurađ and at Placa, Šipanska Luka.

Bus Runs between Suđurađ/Šipanska Luka in line with the ferry schedule (Postira and Vis), six or seven times daily, not Sundays or holidays.

Taxi T: +385 (0)989 563080 or +385 (0)989 042402 (off-road)

Boat moorings There are berths at both Suđurađ and Šipanska Luka, but availability may be difficult in the peak season. Always take advice on the prevailing weather.

ATMs Next to Šipan Hotel in Šipanska Luka.

Surroundings

'Protected from the winds,
Our gardens are embraced by a mild frost,
And the gentle winter does not burn our flowers.'

– Ilija Crijevic

IF YOU'RE PLANNING on staying more than a week or so in the Elaphites, consider hiring a boat: it transforms the islands from tranquil outposts, to an excellent base for exploring the region. First to explore is the rest of the Elaphites. Daksa, just 1.5 nautical miles from Dubrovnik's Gruž harbour, is the smallest island in the archipelago, just 500 metres long and 200 metres wide. It used to have a Franciscan monastery, which briefly housed the senate itself, after a fire destroyed Dubrovnik's Rector's Palace in 1459. It was also the spot where Ivan Gundulič wrote his poem 'Suze Sina Rametnoga' ('Tears of a Prodigal Son'). Later it became a French, then Austrian military stronghold, and then a private island. Today only ruins remain, bar the lighthouse, built in 1873 and still in use. Sadly, it is now remembered for the massacre of 44 men in 1944 – a symbol of the communist regime's crimes against its own citizens.

Sveti Andrija, six nautical miles from Gruž, is a rocky, battered 617-metre-long grey strip, rising sheer from the waves. It too has a lighthouse, built in 1873 and rebuilt several times since, which is one of the most powerful in the Adriatic. Benedictines constructed what must have been a particularly bleak monastery here in the 13th century. Later it was used as a quarantine for diseased mariners from Lopud, and a place for exiles and hermits (Mavro Vetranovič retreated in the mid-16th century and lived here almost to his death 25 years later, writing an autobiographical poem called 'Remeta'). The monastery and other buildings were destroyed by the earthquake that levelled Dubrovnik, and were never rebuilt.

Ruda, an islet opposite Šipan's Suđurad, housed Augustinians briefly in the 16th century, then Dominicans – until it was ravaged by pirates, prompting the monks to decamp to Lopud. Nobody lived there again until the French built a fortress in 1808, which was destroyed by cannon fire from a passing English ship five years later. According to local legend, Ruda was also where concerned islanders dumped an habitually drunk woman to sober up – a sound plan, until a ship laden with wine was wrecked nearby, and its barrels washed up on Ruda's shores... Jakljan is rather more welcoming: a 3.45-square-kilometre island inhabited in summer, it's a tranquil spot, with a good harbour and a beach within a forested bay. It's very close to Šipan, and was historically used as overspill for farming, cattle and fishing. It also has the remains of a 13th-century Benedictine church, called St Izidora.

Tiny Olipa, the last island in the chain, was still inhabited until 30 or 40 years ago. It has a hidden cove with a sandy beach where pirates used to hide, and, perhaps, bury their treasure. On the Pelješac peninsula, just opposite, is the spot where a sailor was washed up on a narrow ledge when his boat sank some 150 years ago. He couldn't swim, and, holding on to a piece of wood, he made a deal with God, promising that if he was saved, he would live wherever he landed for the rest of his life. He lived on that same ledge on a sheer cliff (which you can still see) for 20 years, supplied with food from passing fishermen. When he died, his skeleton stayed put until just before the Second World War, when his bones were at last cast into the sea and his skull was removed for burial.

A little way along the peninsula, where it attaches to the mainland, lie the beautiful fortified towns of Ston and Mali Ston. The latter is on the northern side, with a natural lake-like bay that has been renowned for its mussel and oyster farms since Roman times: their shellfish are served up in the clutch of superb restaurants nearby, making it a gourmand's paradise. The rather bigger, and more historic, Ston is on the south side, surrounded by its amazing wall, second only to China's Great Wall, built to guard the ancient salt pans (which are still being worked today).

Finally, there is Mjlet, directly to the west of Olipa. Nearly three quarters of this 1000 square kilometer island is forest, dotted with vineyards, villages and fields, and fringed with enticing sandy coves. Its whole western side has been a national park since 1960, picked out for its two indented salt-water lakes, surrounded by lush vegetation – a refuge for many animals. A magical place. *ff*

Summer idyll

Dotted around the whole area are flashes of architectural elegance, notably the historic villas, such as Ljetnikovac Sorkocevic (opposite) in Rijeka Dubravacka, now home to Dubrovnik's largest marina. Villas were a statement of wealth, and a means of escaping the hot summer stench and disease of the city. Yet there was concern that spending too much time in their beautiful surroundings might be equally intoxicating: an idyllic, lazy life hard to tear oneself away from. And there is more than a sprinkling of hints in the Renaissance writings that they were also places for amorous intent...

49

A tour of Elaphites' surroundings

A trip northwest up the coast towards Pelješac works best, and is most enjoyable, by sea. Our listings are organised with that in mind, proceeding via historic Ston up to Pelješac from the Elaphites, then returning down the coast back towards Dubrovnik.

Indeed, this route is very much on the boating itinerary, from megayachts (which beat a regular path) down to smaller boats, and even kayaks inshore. Note that if you are travelling by sea, ensure you have a qualified skipper on board, or are otherwise properly prepared and experienced.

Starting from **Šipanska Luka**, travel straight out of the bay past the now uninhabited islands of **Jakljan, Olipa** and their smaller neighbours. The scenery of islands and the backdrop of Pelješac as you approach is majestic, especially at sunset.

To the west is **Mljet,** not truly an Elaphite, but close enough to be at least a cousin. This is a quiet treasure, with its National Park, a 12-square-mile haven of pine and oak forests, steep cliffs and saltwater lakes – it's also the only European home to mongooses (put there to get rid of snakes). In the larger lake lies St Mary's Island, with a 12th-century Benedictine monastery, and Saplunara is one of the finest sandy beaches in the whole of Dalmatia. You can stay on the island too.

Beyond Olipa, the route leads into the beautiful Ston channel and **Kobas Bay.** Approached from the sea on the west side of the channel, this tranquil cove is home to a number of family-run restaurants. Kobas is inhabited by five families throughout the year, living exclusively from fishing, wine and olive production. People are there because they choose to be – owners and customers alike. Expect a warm welcome – and to take your time. 🚤

Tavern Ribarska Kuća On the centre-left of the bay with a good jetty, Nico Bilic and family run this taverna with a steady supply of fresh seafood. There is a wonderful castle/mill just next door.
T: +385 (0)20 754774

Luka's Taverna On the centre-right of the bay, Luka and his family run an equally relaxed and welcoming taverna. Mariners have been coming back for years, decorating the stone walls inside with their boat names. T: +385 (0)20 754771

Continuing up the Ston channel, you'll arrive at **Ston** itself, with its impressive ancient wall (now being refurbished). Ston is at the base of the Pelješac peninsula, stretching north out towards Korčula. Opposite the mainland, the peninsula forms an ideal and extensive sea basin for the cultivation of shellfish at Mali Ston.

There are three restaurants at **Mali Ston**, all well frequented by canny gourmands. Road transport from Dubrovnik can be arranged – it's about an hour's drive along the coastal road.

Hotel Ostrea and Restaurant Kapetanova Kuća The town guard captain's house in the days of the Republic, with a small number of rooms. Run by the Kralj family, who are well-known in Croatia for their cooking. T: +385 (0)20 754555 W: ostrea.hr

Restaurant Bota Adjacent to Kapitenova Kuca.
T: +385 (0)20 754482 W: bota-sare.hr

Villa Koruna: With large fish tanks inside, Villa Koruna has been open for many years. It also has rooms.

T: +385 (0)20 754999 W: vila-koruna.hr

From Ston, venture up into **Pelješac**, the peninsula running up to **Korčula**. We give no more than a brief introduction here, and then only as far as **Dingač**, the breathtaking, impossible near-vertical vineyards that face west towards Mjlet. Pelješac is about wine and agriculture, and is thoroughly focused on its cultivation.

We mention only the village of **Trstenik**, the Dingač coastal gateway. Pause here – the Dingač slopes are just beyond. Then take the ancient mountain tunnel back into the centre, where there are a growing number of winemakers with their cellars. There are organised wine tours, but equally you can just drop in. There are also many smaller cellars too – locals usually top up at these.

Travelling back down the coast from Ston towards Dubrovnik, you come to **Trsteno**, famous for its arboretum with its ancient collection of cultivated and exotic tree species and plants – including two gigantic 500-year-old Asiatic plane trees – spread through a Renaissance park. There are also five old chapels containing valuable paintings besides the Renaissance church St Vid. Trsteno also has a wonderful harbour at the bottom of the cliff, which is accessible on foot or by road.

Further on is **Orasac**, home to the **Sun Gardens Radisson Hotel and Resort**. Originally opened in the 1980s, this large and impressive location looking west over Lopud and Koločep has undergone extensive redevelopment over the last few years. The first hotel, with 201 bedrooms, is due to open in 2009, together with 207 apartments in a resort village, with a variety of restaurants, outlets, beaches and other recreational facilities – all managed by Radisson. Highly significant for the region, this will be the first newly-built resort to international standards, allowing visitors to come to Dubrovnik as they wish but stay outside, to relax and enjoy the region in luxury. The shape of things to come.
T: +385 (0)20 361500 W: radissonblu.com/resort-dubrovnik

Next comes **Zaton Mali**, where you can stop off at:

Restaurant Gverovic-Orsan An old boathouse, now a highly regarded restaurant, on the water's edge just below the road.
T: +385 (0)20 891267 W: gverovic-orsan.hr

From Zaton Mali, it's about a 20-minute drive back to Dubrovnik – or quicker by boat from Orsan's jetty.

53

Dubrovnik

'O beautiful, o beloved, o sweet freedom,
the adornment of the Dubrava.
All silver, all gold, all human lives
cannot match your beauty.'

– Ivan Gundulić

FAMOUSLY DUBBED THE pearl of the Adriatic, Dubrovnik effortlessly lives up to its Byronic moniker, and indeed feels like nothing has changed much since. Inside the hefty medieval walls, which skirt its rocky promontory and can be a whopping 19 feet thick in places, are marble streets and cultural monuments galore, an atmosphere of timelessness that comes from everything being of a piece: a living, breathing (and indeed lively at night) architectural treasure trove. Yet few major destinations in the world have a history that feels quite so close too: it's less than 20 years since two out of three buildings here were hit by shells during the siege by the Yugoslav army.

That seems hard to believe today as you stroll along the famous Stradun, the main street of the Old Town: the restoration since the war ended in 1995 has been painstaking and thorough. The crowds are flocking back here, and it gets very busy in high summer, particularly with visitors from the cruise ships – so get out early and explore before they arrive. The Old Town's market in Gundulić Square, one of the central plazas, is a great place to start. It's a buzz of activity, where you will find all the locals buying and selling their freshly home grown fruit, vegetables, flowers, olive oil, cheese and wine. Then just wander. Mercifully, the Old Town is pedestrian only, with narrow alleys weaving between larger streets punctuated by such architectural gems as the Church of Sv Vlaha, Sponza Palace, Franjevacki Samostan, the Rector's Palace and the Katedrala. If it gets *too* busy, delve deeper and head for the back streets, especially over towards the sea, where you can feel lost in time and see locals still going about their daily business.

For those who know Italy well, Dubrovnik prompts a kind of déjà vu. It all feels so familiar, until some particular detail reminds you that this side of the Adriatic belongs to the Slavs – although many others have made their mark over the years. Founded by refugees from the destroyed Roman city of Epidaurum (now Cavtat) in the 7th century, it has always been an entrepot and cultural melting pot; a mercantile powerhouse that by the 12th century was trading freely in Byzantium, and by the 14th had shaken off the suzerainty of Venice, 'the queen of the sea' – its greatest influence, and also its most hated rival. In 1458, it became tributary of the Ottoman sultan, although it remained largely independent, paying tribute but getting trading rights and closer economic links in return, and generally being allowed to continue being a money-making machine.

In the 15th and 16th centuries particularly, Dubrovnik thrived; a real star in the Renaissance firmament. Yet the seeds of its decline had already been sown, with growing competition and, particularly, the discovery of the Americas causing a regional trade collapse that eclipsed mighty Venice too. Then calamity struck: a devastating earthquake on 6 April 1667 killed more than 5000 citizens, including the prince, and destroyed many buildings, although the walls remained intact. Much of what exists now comes from the rebuilding. The drifting Republic officially came to an end in 1808, becoming part of the expansive French empire, two years after Napoleon marched into the city. The old nobility attempted to rise again a few years later, but it fizzled out – as did the French occupation, and the Habsburgs took over from 1815 to the end of their empire in 1918.

All this history is writ large on the Old Town's evocative streets. But for another view, literally, take a trip up to Srd – the fort high on the hill – and enjoy the spectacular panorama. The fort and cable car suffered during the war, but its few defenders held out, so playing a major role in saving the city. For another view again, visit Lokrum Island, just 15 minutes away by boat, where Richard the Lionheart was said to have been shipwrecked. It has a converted old Benedictine monastery, which created an exotic botanical garden that continues today. As for culture, visit the Modern Art Gallery, past Lazareti beach, for a terrific 20th-century display, including work by the sculptor Ivan Mestrovic and realist painter Vlaho Bukovac. Or come in July and August for the famous Dubrovnik Summer Festival, which boasts a superb programme of drama, opera, music and ballet taking place at open air stages in the Old Town. *ffi*

Complete overview

The walk around Dubrovnik's ramparts is unmissable, offering a panoramic circumnavigation of the Old Town and stunning views of the sparkling sea to boot. Those terracotta tiles, an icon of Dubrovnik, are actually a poignant reminder of the destruction wreaked by the 1991 siege: some are a bit too orange, too monotonous, replacements for the lighter, more varied originals that were destroyed in the bombardment and, alas, were impossible to reproduce.

60

Where to stay

There are many hotels in and around Dubrovnik – but still not enough. The selection here is only for those who want to stay inside or right by the Old Town. Look also for hotels towards Lapad or Gruž, such as Bellevue, Libertas, Dubrovnik Palace or Compas, to name a few, which are a longer walk or taxi ride from the Old Town.

Pucic Palace The only true luxury hotel inside the Old Town itself. Not cheap, but then you are staying in a historic building within the walls themselves. **T:** +385 (0)20 326222 **W:** thepucicpalace.com

Hotel Starigrad Affordable family-run hotel inside the Old Town with good elevated views from its roof terrace. **T:** +385 (0)20 322244 **W:** hotelstarigrad.com

Excelsior Hotel The nearest luxury waterfront hotel to the Old Town, to the south east, a short walk (seven minutes or so) from Ploce Gate. Recently refurbished, yet retaining its roots. **T:** +385 (0)20 353353 **W:** hotel-excelsior.hr

Hotel Argentina Another fine waterfront luxury hotel, just beyond the Excelsior, and with similarly fine views into the harbour end of the Old Town. **T:** +385 (0)20 440555 **W:** gva.hr

Hilton Hotel Opened in 2006 on the site of the old Hotel Imperial, a short walk from the Old Town's northwest Pile Gate. Though not waterfront, it has become well established. **T:** +385 (0)20 320320 **W:** hilton.co.uk/dubrovnik

Look also for **holiday rentals**, particularly renovations in or around the Old Town. Try agents such as Dubrovnik Premium (dubrovnik-ps.hr), Elite (elite.hr) or Gulliver (gulliver.hr).

Where to eat and drink

All these are recommended – as is booking, unless otherwise stated:

Posat Konoba just outside Pile Gate in a lovely setting with a diverse menu, particularly strong on grilled meats. **T:** +385 (0)20 421194

Lokanda Pescarija On the Old Town harbour front, an established fish restaurant next to the fish market. No bookings, just turn up: there are lots of tables, but you may still have to queue a bit. 🛈

Orhan Waterfront restaurant in the atmospheric little harbour just under the Old Town Pile Gate. **T:** +385 (0)20 414183

Kamenice A reliable family-run fish restaurant in Gundulić Square. **T:** +385 (0)20 326682

Gil's Cuisine With a stunning terrace overlooking the Old Town harbour, and an innovative, artistic menu prepared by designer chef, Gilles Camilleri. **T:** +385 (0)20 322222 **W:** gilsdubrovnik.com

Nautika and **Proto** These are established consistent restaurants within (and just outside) the Old Town. **T:** +385 (0)20 442526

Glorijet Next to the Gruž fish and veg market on the edge of the harbour, this is traditional (meat and fish) and one of the best. Sit upstairs at the back. **T:** +385 (0)20 419788 🛈

Komin Literally means 'open fire', Ivo's old-style woodland taverna with traditional menu. In Lapad. **T:** +385 (0)20 435636

Dubravacka Kantun Home-style cooking in the heart of the Old Town. Allow time. **T:** +385 (0)20 331911

Eden Well-known Tonci's traditional charcoal-grill fish restaurant

overlooking Lapad Bay. **T:** +385 (0)20 435133

Festival Cafe to watch the world go by, on Stradun.

Troubador Marko, aging rock star, runs this energetic jazz/live Old Town music bar (an institution) with family, friends and oft-changing, always-talented band. Open all year, indoors in winter, spilling into the atmospheric courtyard in the summer. If you are really good, ask about making a guest appearance in the band – be warned, he has high standards. 🛈

Hole in the Wall, Buza We'll leave you to find it yourself (clue: it's on the sea-front side...). Enjoy a drink at this Old Town favourite, especially a sundowner – there's always plenty of action to keep you amused.

Dubravka Cafe/konoba; sit, drink, eat – watch. Outside Pile Gate.

What to do

Walk the walls If you can, you should, for the best orientation and great views. Unchanged since the 14th century, with various forts along the way. Take water: it's two kilometers, though you can do half if you prefer. There is also a cafe where you can have a breather just before the half-way point.

Cultural monuments The basic list includes the Cathedral, Rector's Palace, Church of St Blaise, Sponza Palace, and the Dominican and Franciscan Monasteries. Consider taking a tour or hiring a guide for the full benefit.

Museums and art galleries These are numerous, and should include the Maritime Museum (St John Fort) and War Photo Limited (signposted about half-way down Stradun).

Art to buy There are many galleries tucked away in the streets. Try Ana and Natasha at Gallery Stradun (on Stradun). If you are serious, ask them to open the upper-floor galleries as well.

Take it in Wander and explore the streets at your leisure. See around the various alleyways, each of which will have some visual point of interest. It's difficult to get truly lost.

Visit **Lokrum Island** See page 91.

Srd Pronounced 'Serj', Srd is the Napoleonic fort atop the hill above the city. Take a taxi to see the stunning panoramic views or sunset there. There's also a museum dedicated to the city's defence during the 1990s siege.

61

'You invite me to your palace on the water,
Where all kinds of ships come ashore,
Where sirens celebrate you in their songs,
Luring you with their caresses into paradise.'

– Maroje Mazibradic

THE ELAPHITES WEAR their history on their sleeve, with remarkably little modern embellishment. Blessed with often fertile soil, an ideal climate, superb natural harbours, abundant waters and proximity to the mainland, these islands were always going to be appealing to the restless peoples of ancient and early history. The Illyrians settled here first, leaving a sprinkling of remains – notably some defensive walls on Šipan. Defence from the sea has always been key in this part of the world, and indeed most of the settlements on these islands began inland, only moving to the coast as their power grew.

The Greeks arrived next, but left little beyond names (Gypanon for Šipan, Kalamota for Koločep, Dalafota for Lopud), and then came the Romans. It was Pliny himself, the illustrious naturalist and philosopher, who literally put the islands on the map, giving them the name they still have today: the Elaphites, or deer islands, either because their shape reminded him of antlers, or because they were then full of fallow deer (nobody is quite sure which). Roman remains include the Villa Rustica in Šipanska Luka, statues from a sarcophagus discovered in Koločep, and the account of the great sea battle between Caesar and Pompey, which may or may not have taken place just off Šipan.

The Slavs arrived in the 7th century, and are still here. By the early middle ages the Elaphites, including Šipan, came under the jurisdiction of the Republic of Ragusa, or Dubrovnik. It was about this time that the numerous pre-Romanesque churches, so characteristic of this part of the Adriatic, began to appear on the islands. Small, simple and deeply atmospheric, they were built as personal acts of piety by wealthy individuals, and reflect a highly developed early Croatian culture. Particularly remarkable early examples, built between the 9th and 11th centuries, include St Anthony of Padua, St Nicholas and St Sergius on Koločep; St Elijah, St John, St Peter and St Nicholas on Lopud; and St Peter on Šipan.

In stark contrast to these is the mighty Sveti Duh (Holy Spirit) on Šipan, a rare example of the Renaissance-Mannerist style, built in the shape of a cross in 1577. A fortress as well as a church, this was where villagers retreated when Šipan was attacked by pirates, an all-too-regular occurrence. Its elaborate series of defences can still be seen – and it still holds services every Sunday.

In the 14th century, the capital of the Elaphites was effectively Šipan, home to the Comes Insularum, the Lord of the Islands, one of six rectors in the Republic, each governing his own principality. The rector was civil and military head, and supreme judge to boot, limited in power only by the all-powerful Dubrovnik senate. He was required to visit Lopud and Koločep, but resided in his official residence in Šipanska Luka. The palace that stands above the town today was built in 1450 – the date is displayed over the entrance, along with a stone sculpture of St Vlaho, the protector of the republic. By the late 15th century, the thriving Republic was reorganised into 10 dukedoms, including one for Šipan, and one for Lopud and Koločep (Ston and Mljet had one each too).

The story of the Ragusan Elaphites is one of prosperity built on maritime commerce that advanced like a tide from Dubrovnik. Koločep prospered first, then Lopud, then Šipan, which experienced its golden age at the peak of the Republic's power, and so has the most remarkable monuments. Just as the tide of prosperity advanced, so it retreated. Dubrovnik started losing its power as Flemish, English and French ships started a direct trade with the Levant, becoming fierce competitors, while the discovery of the Americas led to a trade recession right the way across the Mediterranean.

The Dubrovnik merchants adapted by investing their money in banks, living off their properties' revenues, and renouncing their ships. This led to the growth of crafts: jewellery-making, production of cloth, scarves, glass, soaps, metal and other goods. Turk and Serbian caravans came down to the sea, to purchase supplies there. The people of Dubrovnik could make a living this way, but not the islanders. The tide of prosperity has been receding ever since, but at last it is on the turn, due to carefully planned, sustainable tourism.

A place of sanctuary

The Elaphites are scattered with churches and chapels: Šipan alone has 38, including simple Sveti Petra (St Peter, opposite), built in the 11th century and recently carefully restored. Such pre-Romanesque churches are typical of this part of the Adriatic, and reflect the sophistication of the early Croatian culture. Many rarely, if ever, have services, particularly on the sparsely populated Elaphites, but they are carefully tended by locals, and are sublimely atmospheric places for quiet contemplation.

Glories past and present

Strong hints of past prosperity are evident in the tumbledown exteriors of the many houses, large and small, that await restoration. Occasionally, their past interiors are still there too, and in some cases – notably the foremost Skočibuha castle in Suđurad – considerable preservation work has already been tenderly completed (below). In Šipanska Luka, the house of the Stjepovic family (opposite) is a fine example of more recent wealth. The grandfather of the current owner went to seek his fortunes overseas, leaving as a teenager. His travels eventually took him to Peru where he cornered the nitrate market just before the Boer War – perfect timing as it is a key ingredient for gunpowder. Returning, he lavished his newfound riches on his beloved home island, building a number of houses. Alas, in the largest, someone forgot to design in a kitchen, so they had to bolt it on afterwards. And in the end the construction process was so drawn out that what should have been the top floor was adapted to become another house along the shore.

Patiently waiting

Houses gently falling into disrepair is a feature of the whole region, particularly the islands. Often abandoned by departing residents, it's rather as if they were put on hold. This includes some Renaissance palazzos – 'view' houses, as they were sometimes called – and their mini-estates, some inland, some on the shoreline, as well as smaller houses or even whole villages. Lying in between are the olive groves, terraces and vineyards that went with them.

71

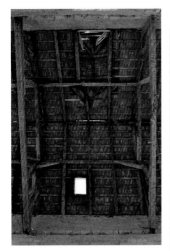

What goes around

The houses in the Elaphites often have a strong Italianate influence, and are rich in artisinal and local details. The pink tone which is so common here is pigmented with horse blood. Due to the general depopulation, many houses – and sometimes whole villages, notably on the larger Šipan – lie abandoned, offering interesting opportunities for renovation. Some of these, in their turn, were originally built from stone salvaged from the ruins of earlier buildings, constructed in the islands' heyday.

Terroir

'A vine needs tending like a wife.
An olive tree waits like a mother.'

– Croatian proverb

BLESSED WITH ENDLESS sunshine, fertile soil and turquoise waters, it's hardly surprising that the food in the Elaphites is abundant, fresh and excellent. Croatian cuisine demonstrates the country's diverse heritage, with robust Slavic flavours inland, particularly in the forested north, and more Mediterranean influences on the coast – notably Italian. Think fresh fish, cured ham, plenty of vegetables, olive oil with everything, homemade cheese, the occasional chunk of grilled meat – and coffee, plenty of it, at all times of the day and night, a legacy of the caffeine-fixated influence of Italy, Turkey and Vienna.

Wine is absolutely fundamental to any meal – the local saying goes that the fish must swim three times: in the sea, in oil and in wine – and many islanders make and drink their own, which they naturally insist is the best available. They've certainly had plenty of practice. Viticulture here goes back to several centuries BC when grapevines were introduced to the Adriatic coast by the ancient Greeks or Phoenicians. At the start of the 20th century, Croatia was a significant player with some 90,000 hectares under vine in Dalmatia alone – as with so much here, this has dropped off significantly, and according to 2005 figures, only 59,000 hectares remain nationally.

Nevertheless, the wine here is good – often surprisingly so – with the potential to be very good indeed. International interest was piqued when it was discovered that Dalmatia is almost certainly the original home of Zinfandel, which is identical to an ancient Croat variety called Crljenak Kaštelanski (Tribidrag). The local red is very much in the Zinfandel vein: big, bold and ripe, with a hefty alcohol content of around 14 to 15 percent, such as the excellent Dingač and Postup on the Pelješac peninsula, and Zlatan Plavac, Ivan Dolac, and Faros on Hvar – all made from the indigenous Plavac Mali grape. White grapes, which make up around a third of production, include: Pošip and Grk on Korčula, Vugava on Vis, Bogdanuša on Hvar and Maraština all along the coast. Pošip and Bogdanuša can produce wines that are fresh, quite light and herbal; the others are deeper, richer, clearly hot climate wines.

Just as important as wine is olive oil, served throughout the meal, both with and on just about everything – there are even oils sweet enough to be served on pudding. Like the vines, olive trees here date back about as far as history goes: archaeological findings of olive stones suggest that they were cultivated in Dalmatia in the 9th century BC. It became so important in the Ragusa Republic that no man could obtain a wedding permit without providing proof that he had planted at least 20 olive trees.

The inhabited Elaphites were the epicentre for Ragusan olive oil production, and crops generally, particularly on Šipan which became known as the bread basket of the Republic. At the start of the 20th century, this island alone had some 500 hectares of olive groves and more than 90,000 trees, all tended lovingly. But as the population declined, so too did production, and a recent survey showed that Šipan today has some 220 hectares of olive groves and 35,000 olive trees. A big drop off – but still a lot of olive trees, particularly for a population that now stands at around 500. (Indeed, Šipan has entered the *Guinness World Records* as the place with the largest number of olive trees in relation to its size and number of inhabitants.)

Olive oil production is back on the rise now across the region, and fabulous groves of ancient trees are being reclaimed. Croatian olive oil has a growing reputation. Like the wine here, a lot of oil is produced, used and, sometimes, sold privately by proud local growers. Even commercial producers are small, and the taste of each oil varies from region to region. Istria is becoming particularly renowned, even in Italy, with four producers listed among the world's top 100. The south is less well known internationally, but has great potential. Dalmatia, and the Elaphites particularly, are capable of producing outstanding extra virgin olive oil, as they always have. Moreover, it is perfectly possible to create an appellation-style geographic distinction for locally produced oils, since these islands are home to six unique cultivars – a rare distinction indeed, demonstrating the rich and unique character of this abundant region. *ff*

Rich harvest

Oranges, lemons, figs and pomegranates are all grown here, as well as the olives and vines. Croatia is home to around 15 or so olive cultivars of which four predominate (Leccino, Buga, Levantika and Oblica – also called Trgonja). In the Elaphites the main cultivar is another, Piculja, which takes longer to mature but is worth the wait. Olives are harvested from October. Modern olive presses have taken over, but old ones still exist, some coated in dust, others carefully preserved.

81

A botanist's dream

The Elaphites are extraordinarily rich in flora. Šipan alone has 617 species, 20 of which are rare or endangered. Throughout the islands you'll find a mix of aromatic plants and flowers, as well as exotics such as palms, agaves and cacti, creating a unique atmosphere. The majority of the species are Mediterranean, and there is much diversity across the varied landscape. Beyond the fertile and cultivated areas, the harsher, rocky landscape boast numerous heathers and natural herbs, such as rosemary, basil, lavender and sage, interspersed with Aleppo pine and cypress.

Catch of the day

Fresh seafood is abundant in these waters and fishing remains one of the main employers in the Elaphites. The clear, clean seas of the Adriatic mean the quality of the catch is high, and it is sold both locally and in Dubrovnik. A local catch might include shrimp, sardines, mackerel, squid, tuna and sea bass. Fish is typically prepared with delicious simplicity, pan-fried in olive oil, grilled on the barbeque or baked.

What to eat

Croatian food blends Mediterranean, Balkan and Central European influences, but if you want a generalisation for comparison, think Italian. Each region has its own distinct style of cooking, with the Dalmatian coast being dominated by fresh fish and seafood. Grilling is a popular form of cooking meat and fish in this region and olive oil is used generously.

The quality of the food substantially reflects the quality of the ingredients. A statement of the obvious, perhaps, but it's particularly apposite here. The seafood comes from crystal clear waters, vegetables are mostly locally grown, and the meat is generally good too. Very often a good meal is simple: with the ingredients so fresh, it's best to let them speak for themselves. That's not to say that there aren't some excellent chefs who can create complex wonders as well. It seems most Croatians are born foodies, and they will speak with passion about the raw materials. Feel free to ask about anything that's been served. Bear in mind too that many foods are available only in season, rather than year round.

Here are a few pointers to what you might find on the menu:

Olive Oil (*maslinova ujlio*) Without doubt, this is a big growth area for Croatia. Many of the oils are simply stunning. It is worth asking to be sure you have the really good oil on the table, although the standard is still generally fine (and will often be the best anyway). If you want to go one step further, ask where the oils are from – in a number of restaurants they pride their 'library' selection and you really can taste the difference between them. Šipan oil is particularly good, if you can get hold of it. Ultimately olive oil may well become treated like fine wines, with good ones being particularly sought after by a growing band of connoisseurs. Also, olive oil is generally regarded as being good for you, so indulge and enjoy.

Cheese (*sir*) There are number of local cheeses. On Šipan, for example, there are only a handful of cows, and some say they can identify by taste which one is responsible for a particular cheese. Try the cheese from the island of Pag, which is more widely available. It is made from milk from sheep fed on the island's copious seaweed. It makes for an exquisite taste. It is expensive, but worth it.

Dried ham (*prsuit*) This comes in varying grades. A common dish as a starter is *prsuit* and *sir*. Combine it with olives and onions too.

Rocket (*rucola*) Generally it has a strong taste here with a particularly 'home-grown' peppery flavour. Delicious.

Fish soup Tends to be good, and is a staple of any family meal.

Shellfish Widely available. See the listings on page 53 for the magnificent shellfish of Ston, where many species are grown.

Squid Fresh from the sea can be very special. Try them grilled.

Vegetables Typically local and excellent, especially grilled.

Garlic Yes, plenty. Allicinophiles will feel at home here.

Asparagus If it's the wild asparagus season (March-May), don't miss out. Wild asparagus looks stringy, but don't be fooled. It's more tasty and delicious than the captive version. Often served simply with scrambled eggs and judging by the scented after effects, its cleansing qualities are potent.

Figs In season (August-November), homemade bags of semi-dried figs are available in markets. Well worth a try.

Octopus salad Don't be alarmed if this is prepared from frozen, as the process makes the octopus more tender.

Seafood risottos Widespread and often excellent, seafood risotto can be made with squid and squid ink, prawns or just about any seafood. Also look out for *buzara* and *brudet* (fish stew).

Meat Dalmatian meat dishes are also popular and include spit-roast lamb (*janjetina*), beef stewed with sweet wine (*pasticada*), steaks and schnitzels.

Pizzas Being just across the water from Italy, pizzas are also widely on offer.

Ice cream (*sladoled*) A must for anyone with a sweet tooth, its rich creamy taste is often offered in a wide range of flavours.

Pancakes (*palacinke*) A popular dessert, served with walnuts, chocolate or jam.

What to drink

The same passion for food extends to wine. Croatian wine is not well known internationally – generally because so far there's limited supply, and it tends to be consumed domestically. However, there are a significant number of wines which are high quality and well worth trying. You really just have to try for yourself or ask for advice. Have a look too at our fuller tasting notes on page 79.

The Pelješac region is probably the best known for producing good red wine: **Dingač**, **Postup** and **Plavac Mali** (although the Plavac can be quite heavy). Mato at **Matusko** (pictured opposite, in his cellar) produces consistently good Pelješac wines including Dingač and Postup. T: +385 (0)20 742393 on some of the tours and worth a visit.

For a good white, try a well-chilled bottle of **Pošip**. Or ask for a white Malvazija – recently in Paris, **Konalvoska Malvazija** (from just south of Dubrovnik) achieved one of the highest ever ratings for this type of wine. Malvazija is a medium rather than dry wine.

Herbal grappa is often served as an aperitif, and generally claimed to have medicinal properties. You may agree. There's also **Prosek**, a sweet red regional wine, served before or after the meal.

For lager, **Karlovacko** and **Ozujsko** are the main local brews.

Left to right, top to bottom

1. **Fresh octopus:** Evening catch at Šipanska Luka.
2. **Matusko welcome:** Mato in his cellars near Dingač, on Pelješac.
3. **Daisy, perhaps:** One of Šipan's five cows.
4. **Tending the *polje*:** Niko walking among his vines.
5. **Maslinova uljio:** Don't miss out on the high quality and wide variety of olive oil available here.
6. **Fresh today:** Just in time for dinner.
7. **Slab happy:** The fish market at Gruž.
8. **A perfect picnic:** Watching the sun set.
8. **Šipan's vineyards:** It's hot work out there.
9. **Radish aforethought:** Vegetable market at Gruž.

Arriving and getting around

Arrival by Air Dubrovnik's international airport is 23 kilometers to the south of Dubrovnik itself, at Cilipi (about three kilometers south of Cavtat). The inward flightpath tracks southeast just off the coast, so if you want excellent views and orientation as you arrive (including Dubrovnik's Old Town), chose a window seat on the left of the plane.

The airport is undergoing a substantial investment programme in order to accommodate the increasing traffic. The number of carriers flying to Dubrovnik is steadily increasing.

When you arrive, you can rent a car or take a taxi or bus into town. Normally, it's a 20-30 minute journey by car or taxi (plentiful), longer (though cheaper, of course) by bus, and longer still if it's high peak summer. If you're hiring a car, it's difficult to get lost as there is only one road, the coastal E65: turn right out of the airport heading north. Be warned, in summer traffic can be heavy. Stop in a layby if you can, for your first glimpse of the Old Town.

Getting around Dubrovnik consists of the Old Town, and then, going northwest, Lapad and Gruž (where the main harbour is). The best way to get around Dubrovnik's Old Town is to walk, especially in the peak season. Going out of the Old Town, the bus system is good, and there also are plenty of **taxis** (best found in the ranks outside Pile Gate towards the Hilton Hotel, but also outside Ploce Gate). There are ferry boats from the Old Town Harbour too. English is widely spoken, so don't be afraid to ask for help.

In and around the Elaphites

The main terminus for all ferries and boats is the harbour at Gruž.

Jadrolinija is Croatia's national ferry company. *Postira* (opposite) is the workhorse boat in their fleet: it has been operating the Elaphites schedule since the 1950s. The service is regular, between Gruž, Koločep, Lopud, and Suđurađ and Šipanska Luka on Šipan. *Postira* is a legend, and recommended. Boat handling is impressive and tight to timetable.  Jadrolinija also operates a larger ferry, *Vis*, to Šipan (making it overall the island best served) and Mljet.

In total, there are up to five sailings a day. Allow *Postira* half an hour to get you to Koločep, 50 minutes to Lopud, and just over an hour to Suđurađ. She then goes on to and stops overnight at Šipanska Luka. Jadrolinija has many services further afield, operating a comprehensive service amongst many of Croatia's island's, with hubs at Dubrovnik, Split, Zadar and Rijeka, and also connects with Ancona and Bari in Italy. See schedules, or **W:** jadrolinija.hr

Nona Ana A 200-seater privately operated catamaran sailing a high-speed route of Dubrovnik (Gruž), Šipanska Luka, Mljet (Sobra and Polace), Korčula and Lastovo. The schedule is subject to change and doesn't always stop at Šipanska Luka, so best to check.
T: +385 (0)20 313119 **W:** gv-line.hr/linije.php

Hidden Croatia Marine Privately run with local skippers, HCM provides a range of premium excursion and speedboat charter services within the Elaphites. Itineraries are based around a dedicated fleet of quality fast boats, and you can explore the region either privately or in small packaged groups. HCM can also host corporate events. Not surprisingly their programmes almost always include at least one good restaurant (all of which are in our listings).

HCM also operates a private taxi and charter service. (See photographs opposite bottom left and right)
T: +385 (0)20 478880 **W:** hiddencroatiamarine.com

Other private operators It's usually possible to charter small boats with a qualified skipper, and they generally operate out of Gruž or the ACI marina at Rijeka Dubravacka beyond. Ask locally.

Lokrum The small wooded island a short distance from Dubrovnik Old Town Harbour, where Richard the Lionheart is said to have been shipwrecked. The island boasts a converted Benedictine monastery with a botanical garden full of exotic plants, notably many cactus and eucalyptus varieties. A path leads all the way around the island, including to the Mrtvo More, a little sea-water lake and also to the Fort Royal built by the French, which has spectacular views. The island is owned by the state: no individual wants it, thanks to an alleged curse which has led to the early demise of all owners over the past few hundred years.

An hourly ferry goes from the Old Town Harbour during daylight, though the schedule is seasonal, so check first.

Tirena A replica 16th-century Dubrovnik galleon (but with diesel engine and flushing loos) operating out of the Old Town Harbour with excursions throughout the region. Whole, half-day or evening cruises (sunset around the city walls). Watch out for pirate surprises, consorts, sword-play, fireworks and stowaways (not necessarily in that order). **T:** +385 (0)20 358200 **W:** tirena.com

Taxis These are available for long as well as short journeys. They can be booked for the day to include tours further afield, say to Ston or Pelješac. Agree fares beforehand, and check that your driver speaks good English (which most do). Main ranks around the Old Town are outside the main Pile or Ploce Gates.

Please note: This is not intended as a comprehensive listing, though we hope it covers a lot. Schedules are subject to change without notice. There are many online and other sources of information on services available, and new ones are being set up all the time. Please ask and check locally as well.

Go with the ffloe

Our aim is to introduce you to the place and give you some ideas – the raw ingredients so you can work out a trip of your own. Or if you prefer to have someone do that for you, you can point them to things in this book that you want included.

Organising your trip Have a look through the book, particularly the listings, to get ideas. (There's further information on this page too, and also on our website, ffloe.com.) So, if you want to organise your trip directly, you can go straight ahead. Alternatively, if you prefer someone to organise it for you, then we suggest our recommended travel partner, Original Travel (T: +44 (0)20 7978 7333 or W: originaltravel.co.uk). Although we are completely independent, we like Original Travel because, apart from being good people, they have a similar philosophy about travel to our own. There are also other tour operators for the region if you prefer.

When to go

The Croatian coast is blessed with a fine Mediterranean climate. Dubrovnik is at the southern end of the Dalmatian coast, roughly level with just north of Rome, and gets hot weather and a long season. The islands fare even better with micro-climates of their own. There can be clouds over the mainland, yet the islands remain clear.

This is not an area, however, where sunshine is guaranteed – but poor weather rarely lasts long.

The main summer season is like any other in the Mediterranean. However, the 'shoulder' seasons of April/May and September/October are just as good, and some (including us) would say better. In April/May everything is bursting into flower and September/October benefits from the harvests, including the beginnings of the olive oil season. Plus there are fewer people around.

Itineraries

Usually, we all tend to base our holidays around the time we have available, and our budget. However, in this case we recommend a third element – the number of venues that can be fitted in.

This region is made for the excitement of journeys, explorations and discovery – even if those expeditions last for just a single day. There's something to see or experience around every corner, and people here will encourage you to make the most of your time.

Dubrovnik is not large, and will generally hold your attention for two or three days, after which you'll be curious to see more. So either stay there to start off with, and then move on; or stay outside, but have the means to visit it as and when you want (including enjoying at least one evening/night experience inside the walls).

Short break (three days) Almost certainly you'll want to see and experience Dubrovnik, particularly if it's your first time. The obvious option therefore is to stay in or around the Old Town or greater town (Lapad/Gruž) for the whole visit, and make at least one day trip out.

If you've been here before, then perhaps stay outside on the islands or mainland so that you can visit from there. That would mean Koločep, Lopud, Suđurađ (Šipan) or perhaps Sun Gardens at Orasac.

Longer short break (four/five days) There's nothing wrong with staying in Dubrovnik throughout, but if that's your choice, we encourage you to be adventurous. Make sure you explore the region for a full day at least once. Go to Suđurađ, for example. Walk across Šipan, coming back later from Šipanska Luka (take a toothbrush, though, as you may be tempted to stay).

More easily, we advise you to stay in two places, one of which to be anchored in Dubrovnik. If this is your first visit, we suggest you do that to start off with.

A week or more If you've not been here before, then make sure you include at least one or two nights in or around Dubrovnik. You may want to do this first, as arriving from the airport, the city will be in front of you and you'll want to see it.

Thereafter, we advise going further afield, staying in one or even two other places. If that includes a mainland element, consider hiring a car, even for a few days. The coast road is stunning, and it will allow you to take a day out into Pelješac, or south into Konavle.

Obviously, if you are renting a villa or apartment for a week, then you'll want to stay there. Even so, we would encourage you to take at least a day out to explore. Even better, hire a boat for a few days and travel between the islands. That way you'll really get a taste of life here, and have a lot of fun at the same time.

ffloe-rate

We ffloe-rate a small number of venues and experiences that we think you are likely to find particularly memorable and enjoyable. We use our own criteria for these, and it's not just about price either. We expect the service to be good, and certainly sufficient. But thereafter, our key criteria relate to the experience itself.

We have ffloe-rated the following, all of which have the symbol next to them in the listings:

Villa Ruza, restaurant, Koločep (page 27)
Obala, restaurant, Lopud (page 27)
Bozica Hotel, Suđurađ (page 43)
Konoba Kod Marko, restaurant, Šipanska Luka (page 43)
Tauris, restaurant, Šipanska Luka (page 43)
Kobas Bay, Ston Channel (page 53)
Lokanda Peskarija, restaurant, Old Town Harbour (page 61)
Marko's Troubador, jazz cafe, Old Town (page 61)
Glorijet, restaurant, Gruž Harbour (page 61)
Postira, island ferry (page 91)
Hidden Croatia Marine, private boating (page 91)

93

ffloe

Dubrovnik and the Elaphites
Heart of the Adriatic Riviera

First published 2009 by Lowell Limited
PO Box 20, Albury, Guildford, Surrey GU5 9AG, United Kingdom
http://www.ffloe.com

ISBN 978-0-9562844-1-9
Printed and bound in the United Kingdom.

The maps in this book are not cartographically accurate. They are intended as illustrati representations and should be treated as such, and not relied upon for navigation.

ffloe™ Trade mark applied for.

The authors would like to thank all those who have helped and contributed in the preparation of this book, in particular Alen Musan, and also Damir Fabijanic and Caroline, together with Ariana Lusic, Bozo Palunko, Carol and Kuzma Stjepovic, Frano Bezic, Guy Maranzana, Ian Wood, Ivica Katic, Ivan Bavcevic, Ivo Radovic, Ivo Prka, Julian Houchin, Just a Little Light (Live), Luka, Marko and Gino Prizmic, Marko Breskovic, Mato Violic, Miro Ivankovic, Niko Bilic, Nikola Pavlovic, Oliver Beidenegl, Robert Lyle, Rudjer Jelavic, Simon and Felicity Newnes, Stanley Stjepovic, Teo Bogdar Vicki Gerber, William Crewdson, William fforde, Zan Zanetic.

For full listings and locations of the photographs in this book, please visit ffloe.com

If you know of a special place in the world you want us to take a look at or think we should write about, please contact us at travel@ffloe.com, whether you're an individu traveller, resident, hotelier, tourist office or other stakeholder in a region. Our aim is help sustain these places for the future.

GO WITH THE *ffloe*

www.ffloe.com